# THE PORTAGE POETRY
## SERIES

Series Titles

*Sparks and Disperses*
Cathleen Cohen

*Holding My Selves Together: New and Selected Poems*
Margaret Rozga

*Lost and Found Departments*
Heather Dubrow

*Marginal Notes*
Alfonso Brezmes

*The Almost-Children*
Cassondra Windwalker

*Meditations of a Beast*
Kristine Ong Muslim

Praise for
## *Bone Country*

"In *Bone Country*, Linda Nemec Foster's fractured and melancholic travelogue, the poems (or micro-lyric essays) serve as such luscious and destabilizing portals through which the cities of our world are passed, emerging on the other side slick with luminescence—more amazing, more sad, holy, essential, and strange. These poems are magic tricks and ghostly reminders: missives from a not-so-distant, but unreachable past, from places that feel both ultra-real, and wildly imaginary. Not since I read Calvino's *Invisible Cities* for the first time, or discovered the early films of Jim Jarmusch, have I felt the actual world so beautifully defamiliarized, have I been so mystified by the seemingly quotidian dirt under my feet."

—Matthew Gavin Frank
author of *Flight of the Diamond Smugglers*

"In Linda Nemec Foster's *Bone Country*, each keenly composed and compressed piece seems at once fragmented and yet self-contained. It's the speed and addictive rhythm with which they reel by that transforms this collection into a visionary travelogue."

—Stuart Dybek
author of *Ecstatic Cahoots* and *Paper Lantern*

"*Bone Country*, Linda Nemec Foster's thirteenth collection, shimmers with consummate artistry. This treasury of gorgeous and evocative writing is the work of a virtuoso, consistently compelling and a must-read, especially for connoisseurs of the prose poem."

—Clare MacQueen
editor/curator of *MacQueen's Quinterly*

"Based on haunting chance encounters, photographs, and journal entries, the accomplished prose poems in *Bone Country* are Linda Nemec Foster's postcards to the world from her extensive travels, especially in Central and Eastern Europe—a region that reflects her heritage and to which she is deeply connected. Some poems contain the richly layered palette of paintings and tapestries; others capture the briefest lyrical moments: a tree filled with stork nests against the bare sky, the color of a necktie purchased for one's beloved. Still others introduce characters ranging from a perfume salesgirl to an emaciated tour guide to a streetcleaner who moonlights as a performance artist. Recreating the delirious, dreamlike experience of travel across time zones, Foster sometimes sees loved ones in the faces of strangers halfway across the world. She is the ideal traveling companion: compassionate, smart, and keenly observant. Let her take your hand as you travel through *Bone Country*. You'll return changed, in the best possible ways."

—Kathleen McGookey
author of *Instructions for My Imposter*

"Like a lyrical 'missed connections' column of elegantly detailed encounters across the globe, the prose poems of *Bone Country* tantalize and explore the dislocation of traveling through time and mind and place. Our final destination is the dizzying, magical sensation of living as both stranger and familiar friend, of ultimately seeing that we have become 'a single line of pure horizon connecting everything.'"

—Leslie Pietrzyk
author of *Admit This to No One*

# Bone Country

*Prose Poems*

## Linda Nemec Foster

Cornerstone Press
*Stevens Point, Wisconsin*

Cornerstone Press, Stevens Point, Wisconsin 54481
Copyright © 2023 Linda Nemec Foster
www.uwsp.edu/cornerstone

Printed in the United States of America by
Point Print and Design Studio, Stevens Point, Wisconsin

Library of Congress Control Number: 2022947736
ISBN: 979-8-9869663-1-1

Cover art: Albert Bierstadt. *Mountain Brook*, 1863. The Art Institute of Chicago.

Cornerstone Press titles are produced in courses and internships offered by the
Department of English at the University of Wisconsin–Stevens Point.

DIRECTOR & PUBLISHER     EXECUTIVE EDITOR
Dr. Ross K. Tangedal        Jeff Snowbarger

SENIOR EDITORS
Lexie Neeley, Monica Swinick, Kala Buttke

PRESS STAFF
Alyssa Bronk, Grace Dahl, Patrick Fogarty, Angela Green, Cal Henkens, Brett Hill,
Ryan Jensen, Julia Kaufman, Hunter Kiesow, Adam King, Amanda Leibham, Maria
Scherer, Abbi Wasielewski

*To Tony,*
*my best traveling companion.*
*Always.*

Also by Linda Nemec Foster:

*The Blue Divide*
*The Lake Michigan Mermaid*
  (with Anne-Marie Oomen and artist Meridith Ridl)
*The Elusive Heroine: My Daughter Lost in Magritte*
*Talking Diamonds*
*Ten Songs from Bulgaria*
*Amber Necklace from Gdańsk*
*Listen to the Landscape*
*Contemplating the Heavens*
*Living in the Fire Nest*
*Trying to Balance the Heart*
*A Modern Fairy Tale: The Baba Yaga Poems*
*A History of the Body: Prose Poems*

# Contents

# Tea in Istanbul

Men stand outside every restaurant, every store, every fruit stand, enticing you—at times, assaulting you—to come in and buy anything: an exclusive hand-woven carpet, genuine red leather slippers, a bottle of water. I walk past a handsome and hip man standing by the front door of the Historic Angel House Hotel & Restaurant. His spiked mohawk defies gravity, greased and slick. He laughs to himself as if he knows this hawking routine is a joke without a punchline. But he has to do it—the entry level job—before he can work the inside labyrinth of bell boy, night desk clerk, restaurant manager. He wears black leather pants and doesn't act insulted when I pass by quickly, without a second glance. That night, I steal away to the bar next door to the Historic Angel House and drink the liquid amber of Turkish tea. I watch him.

## Conjuring Her Face

The famous artist from Serbia says she looks familiar: he's seen her face in a Belgrade café. She's never been to Belgrade. "That doesn't matter," he replies. He's seen her face—the square jaw, the high cheekbones, the way her eyes scan a room for the nearest exit. He's sketched her a hundred times sipping strong black tea in glass cups, poring over a literary journal filled with oblique poems, impatiently waiting for her lover to stop talking on his cell phone. He's conjured her face with light pastels and translucent watercolors, layered acrylics and misted charcoal, blue pen and sharp pencil. He's memorized every nuance of her expression, every outline she exhales on the pages of his sketchbook. "Look at these," he shows her, "I know you." Eventually, she starts to believe the evidence. As if she never lived her life, as if the blood of her ancestors never left his country.

# In the Old Town, Warsaw

The two policewomen wear mini-skirts and black stilettos and talk constantly; the old woman with the hunched back and iridescent red hair; the young child tethered with the yellow plastic harness to his silent mother; the bored street vendor selling collapsible multi-colored spheres filled with air; the man in the blue shirt, comfortable with his armless torso; the homeless woman in the church vestibule feeling the wooden legs of the crucified Christ and wanting to believe they are real; the crippled man obsessively rubbing his fingers with holy water; the effusive expatriate who used to live in Detroit and now owns a fashionable café. "Anyone can be anybody in this part of the reinvented world," he says to you with your borrowed map and permanent stare. "You should try it."

## Portrait of the Dead

Two things inhabit Warsaw: the green of the summer trees and the persistent spirits of the dead. Each ghost stands guard over each trunk as a silent witness, not to sweeping history, but to daily miracles. A tree gathers rings that mark each year's passing: harsh white of winter becoming soft green of spring. A child, feared dead, reappears at his front door to embrace his astonished mother. The ghosts don't know the details. They only know their duty: pilgrims in the vast green spaces of a once dying city. They lean into the branches' shadows and scatter like seeds above the city's broken horizon. Icons in a group portrait—their faces blank, upturned, to the camera's unwavering eye.

## My Husband Disguised as a Stranger in a Kraków Bar

All the men sit by themselves at small booths that hide the contour of their bodies. Only their pale faces are partly visible because of the cigarette smoke, dark glasses, and casual hand covering a mouth, a left cheek, a sullen forehead. All of them look away, as if they want to be somewhere else. But not him, the man closest to the camera's eye, the man who looks like my husband disguised as a stranger. He stares straight at me. He knows that I know he knows. Something about his past. Exactly how he got that too-perfect nose, the blue-gray eyes when his family's gene pool said brown. What is the legend behind why he parts his hair on the left? What is the great mystery behind why his beard grew in red when the hair on his head was blond then brown then ash—growing from baby to boy to man? I imagine a life for him: a professor of philosophy at Jagiellonian University, parents dead, nicely furnished upper flat on a side street near the Market Square. And no wife in sight. Not until I snap the picture and his stare matches my own.

## Blank Window, Deserted Building, Bratislava

My empty eye has seen it all: the outer landscape of changing seasons—vibrant greens; burning reds; stark grays; tentative shadow of hesitant bloom. Their combined silence never spoke a word. But the man and the woman trapped inside my frame—they whispered and shouted their narrative every day. The man's dark moans, even when he slept. His dreams of childhood trees escaping through the walls. The woman's daily rituals of strong coffee in the morning, stronger plum wine at night. Her loneliness, a constant static floating through the neighbor's hanging laundry. Their unborn child—lost, not expecting anything but air—flickering beyond my field of vision.

# Abandoned House in the Tatra Mountains

Only the foundation is left. Roof, floors, ceilings, walls—all gone. Only the sky remains and the chaotic chorus of wildflowers: dark chicory, red poppies, the slash of willow gentian, chamomiles, blue cornflowers, dog roses, wild angelica in clusters of near white, yarrow crowded into bursts of light purple. They all shout, all at once, from the exposed cellar—as if to sing for no one but each other. Can you hear them? Understand their singular language that will haunt your next dream?

# Planting Geraniums on Geranium Street

She finally lives in the house of her dreams on the street of her childhood in southern Poland. The new house built by her husband in a field close to her parents' old place. The field of her girlhood reticence surrounded by birch and chestnut trees, sparrows, and the laughter of her brother's children. But something is missing from this idyllic tableaux. If the patron saint of luck can't be enticed to stay, she will conjure up the patron flower of loyalty to protect the street: geraniums of strength and forgiveness, geraniums of humility and courage, geraniums of patience and perseverance, of witness and uprising. They have seen everything and yet still continue to grow. So she plants them—talismans, charms, sentinels—all around the house in every shade of red, coral, pink, purple, yellow, blue. The flowers radiant near the white trunks of the birches. Color surrounds every inch of the yard until it shimmers like the wings of a crane. A vision that even the gray sky marvels at with long, silent sighs.

# In the Perfume Store, Kraków

Where did she come from: the girl who sells expensive perfume at a posh store near the Market Square? Nowy Sącz, Rzeszów, Tarnów...any place that's not fashionable. But the consequence of her birthplace does not deter her resolve to know everything about every fragrance ever bottled. From Chanel No. 5 to Gucci's Envy; from the metallic aerosol of Yves Saint Laurent's Rive Gauche to the cobalt blue of Evening in Paris; from Hugo Boss' clean style to the anonymous cologne her grandmother wore. It smelled of strong lilacs and lilies-of-the-valley. The fragrance of purple and white—if colors could exude a smell. That was the girl's first lesson in memory. How certain smells reminded her of certain people. The lesson she remembers every day as she sits in her shop waiting for you and your exposed wrist, the quiet hollow of your neck.

## Our Lady of the Clouds
## Appears Over the Baltic Sea

When Lithuania is locked in nothing but rain, the people pray to Our Lady of the Clouds: the woman born with clouds growing inside her body as nonchalantly as cells or plasma. Stratus, cumulus, and those thin strands of white you hardly notice. Imagine a woman with pure vapor in her bones, the scarves of the wind in her bloodstream. As miraculous as a virgin giving birth to God's son. And what happens when Our Lady of the Clouds answers the people's prayers? Only this...her body of clouds disappears, evaporates, until nothing is left but brilliant blue.

# November Night, Warsaw, 1944

Total darkness: no stars, no moon. As if an entire universe with its roiling planets, imploding supernovae, blinding light years of cosmic dust had abandoned this place and covered it with antimatter. Only one solitary tree—a maple? an oak?—still stands. An unwilling witness to the unraveling of the creation myth. And on the tree, one solitary leaf—glistening with rain? with tears?—bribes the witness to testify. To the beginning, to the end, to the limited possibilities of a muted, endless winter.

## Somewhere in Europe, Surrounded by Villagers, a Bride Leaves Her Home

It could be anywhere. Anywhere after a war where so many fathers, mothers, sisters, brothers died. Or were vanished like thin clouds evaporating into the horizon. The bride feels every absence in her life—contours of faces and shadows of houses. She imagines the black and white of her wedding photo, as if fog cloaked the distant mountains, as if her groom was a ghost that haunted the valleys. The group of quiet observers surrounds her and tries to erase any loss: her worried mother, a somber young boy fingering a worn scarf, the middle-aged man ready to sing with his dark hat. The bride gathers her stiff white wedding dress in each hand (the dress that was made from plain cotton and rows of tatting by her grandmother, the dress that glows like an oasis of light in this long procession) and starts the slow journey to her new life. Who can give her directions? The fashionable shoe on her mother is preoccupied. The groom can barely remember his name. Maybe that young girl with dark bangs and delicate hands knows the way.

# A Child Paints a Snail in the Prague Ghetto, 1942

We don't know the child's name or if the young artist is a boy or a girl. But we see a yellow spiral and a gray head with two antennae. The beach overwhelms the snail's thin, iridescent path and completely dominates the picture—all sand, all light brown—from top to bottom. The scene doesn't even break for the horizon. And neither does the small hand painting it. In this land-locked country, the child can only imagine where sea and sky converge, the waves of the mother's voice singing a path to the invisible stars.

## Gallery of the Street

What words would the lone tree on the corner of Kraków's Market Square speak if it could bear witness to the calculations of war, the liquidation of the city's ghetto? A howl, a whisper, a grunt, a sigh. No words to explain the last defiant shout: the shuffle, shuffle, stomp. Years later, the silence is collected in a cramped museum on the city's edge. The labyrinth of exhibits, the hushed sounds of the lost.

Chopin and Verdi, Bach and Mozart—all emanate from the six strings of a young man's guitar. He could be from Budapest or Prague, Warsaw or Kyiv. All origins of birth lead to the same place—here—in front of the startled eyes of the tourist from LA who tries to adjust to the time zone. The air on this side of the world lifts music to his ears and holds it there like a shell.

The woman with the shaved head is consumed by the art of the street vendor who sells sculptures near the bus station filled with distracted commuters. She wants to be one of his creations: a burlap shroud, a faceless mask. It's a skin she could feel comfortable wearing like a snake in the Garden of Eden. Meanwhile, in the mountains south of the city, her husband waits for her return and counts each cloud as it leaves the sky.

The bent man looks as if he's balancing the whole world on his shoulders. He's mute as the color of dry dust. He can't imagine the idea of garnet, topaz, opal, sapphire. Colors not in his lexicon, not in his sense of geography. He dreams himself into a statue, a piece of granite devoid of movement. Except for a heart beating like a small red fist, glowing in the broken torso.

# On St. James' Feast Day,
# The Shells of Abakanowicz

*—for Denise*

Years before the Polish artist died of dementia and solitude,
the American comes face to face with Magdalena's body of
work in the National Museum in Kraków. "*...and here was
a huge, magical thing...a foreign tongue,*" the artist seems
to whisper in her ear over the text of the gallery notes.
The human and non-human. The endless procession of
life and death: a forest of headless torsos, curved burlap
trees, birds frozen in aluminum. Her obsessive need to
work in the midst of the Nazi boot, the Soviet fist. Here
is the hand-like tree of wire designed for Hiroshima. The
fabric cocoons deposited in New York, as if a butterfly
with amnesia landed on the wrong continent. Here are
the hollowed shells abandoned on a Baltic shore. And
now—a portrait, no, a death mask: eyes shut, a primitive
cross transgressing the face's grid, a primordial landscape,
remnant of bark, leaves, stones, mud. And finally, the
huge fabric tree with tangled roots of twine, bird bones. A
Mazovian willow caught in a storm. The American feels
like a child swallowed whole by that trunk. Smell of musk,
deep pubis, birth canal—a tunnel connecting the pre-life
to the human place in the world. She is childless. The she
of the artist, the she of the observer. But they both know
the journey: having never met, they walk it together.

# The Muslim Wife at the Best Western, Zurich

She wants to be swallowed by the hotel lobby and who can blame her. One day out of Amman and she's breathless, overwhelmed by the exposed skin of other women. Her husband ignores her; he would rather argue with the desk clerk over the weekend rates like he does with the vendors over shoes at the outdoor market of Souk Jara. Without looking at his wife, he tells her to sit in a corner. Swirls of the night sky of the desert inhabit the fabric covering her body. She dissolves into it. Impossible for the Zurich sun to penetrate. Only the sound of her husband's loud demands can get through. What she wants right now is not a hotel room, but the smell of cut lemons from her mother's orchard in the Jordan River valley. Her nostrils breathe the pungent air and she forgets everything: his voice, his skin, his mouth against her bare breast.

# Gemini Marks the First and Second Hour

In the huge brick church in Gdańsk—just to the left of the main altar with its ornate triptych—you can see a medieval clock that marks the hours with the signs of the zodiac. My husband and I look like the Gemini twins who announce the first and second hour. There we are holding hands and offering each other loaves of bread. At the center of the clock's face are the sun, moon, and stars. Signs of the water bearer, ram, fish, and bull float around the clock as if in some imagined and pagan night sky: Scorpio of my son, Leo of my daughter, Virgo of my mother, Libra of my father. Astrology holds center stage. Where does one belief system go when another takes its place? Does it retreat underground, or does it mark the hours near the high altar on the edge of the Baltic Sea? Even the Black Madonna, posing with her Son for the tourists, can't answer the questions. She's assigned a side chapel while another man and woman grow from the serpent's tree in the Garden of Good and Evil.

# Weightless

They could almost touch them, those mountains they only dreamed about as children. Yet here they are in central Switzerland smack in the middle of the Alps. Stylish, haughty, Europe's jagged crevices. So unlike the friendly Green of Vermont, the rambling Appalachian, even the tall but approachable Rockies. Here, the mountains don't care if you notice them or not. Their snow, still blinding and untouched by sun-melt. Their 20-mile tunnels unfazed by his claustrophobia. Their thin waterfalls, indifferent to the tourists' endless gaze, the obligatory photo ops. The husband clutches the steering wheel of the rental car with hands as white as glacial cliffs. The wife stares out the window, dumbstruck and dumbfounded. Her eyes so glazed with the immense and cold beauty, she feels weightless. Like a cloud giving birth to the shadow in the valley below.

# Indigo Sky Above Spain

This morning, clouds spilled from the top of the Sierra Centrales and she remembered the dream she had last night. A childless friend she's known for years finally becomes pregnant. A pink bassinet waiting in the hallway. The husband appears in the background reciting the mantra: "bigger house, bigger house, bigger house." Meanwhile, the road outside their small apartment transforms itself into a long gray ribbon bordered by gorse. The brilliant yellow flowers held in place by tangled branches of thorns. Their scent is like the vague memory of loosestrife, black-eyed Susan, evening primrose that the woman left back home.

The night after witnessing her first bullfight in Seville, she drinks sangria until dawn in a small bar on Calle Arfe. Alone. Quiet. Undisturbed. The locals give her wide berth and cross themselves when passing. Perhaps she is the reincarnation of Carmen returning to haunt their nights. When she finally collapses into her small hotel bed, she dreams of the bullfighter caressing the bull. The horns barely touching the man's body. His cape exploding over the bull's head like a huge blossom of color. Gold, fuchsia, and magenta falling like petals into the open mouths of the amazed tourists.

The last dream before she leaves. The delicate hands of the flamenco dancer who commutes every day from the small village in the Andalusia hills. His narrow, intense face is lost in *duende*; he doesn't even notice her, with her rouge and lip gloss. Another anonymous face in the audience. He is pure gypsy and has the olive skin, long hair, and black eyes to prove it. She has nothing but a faded passport and a husband sleeping alone on the other side of the world. Not even the moon bothers to appear in the indigo sky. Stars shape a new constellation from a myth she will forget by morning.

# Tower of Babel

*"What can we do? The Tower of Babel*
*has done this to us."*
—Wisława Szymborska

I wish I could understand the constant whir of foreign words floating around me on this transatlantic flight—the red-eye following the path of dawn—heading straight to Warsaw, the heart of Europe. Behind me, nothing can stop the three Polish women and their cascade of words: a singing river. I would love to jump in, but I can't swim. Traveling with her mother, a young black girl—maybe 10 or 11—sits beside me, her hair elaborately braided with yarn into rows of purple/red/orange/blue. A foreigner— as opposed to me, with my Slavic face. And yet, I feel a deeper kinship with her (as we joke about reality shows and Chicago hot dogs) than the three women laughing in Polish who could be my grandmothers. Me, the prodigal granddaughter, returning to the land of her ancestors whose language she doesn't know.

## The Waterfall in the Mountains

The young boy loves the waterfalls in Silesia. He can never get enough of the tumultuous sound of water flowing over rocks. "Turn on the faucet in the mountains—more and more," he cries. His mother can only give him stones to throw into the pooling ponds. She can say "I love you" in six different languages. Not enough, never enough. Tomorrow they go back to the gray of Katowice. Tomorrow the mother will offer him nothing but her arms, quiet and empty.

## Flight to Warsaw

The woman with a tiny arm deformed by thalidomide waves to her husband before she enters the security checkpoint. He waves back, not embarrassed by her small, foreshortened gesture. A gesture that would glow in any Renaissance painting by an anonymous monk. But she's flying to Warsaw, not Florence. Warsaw—where all perspective is skewed by Swedish invasions, battles with Teutonic Knights, the Nazi flood, and the Soviet drought. How else to explain the woman's arm in the context of history? How else to understand her husband's faithfulness despite the absent ring, the missing left hand?

# My Tower of Babel

Dear Cousin Maria of the Red and Exotic Painted Toenails...I didn't know your language on that first trip to Poland and I don't know it now. You talk to me in your lilting voice as if I understand every word you're saying, but our vocabularies can't fit into each other's mouths. Like shoes that are too tight, too loose, too narrow, or too wide. We are Cinderella's stepsisters: the girls who can't get the glass slipper to fit. "Such a loss, such a pity," your son Pawel (who knows five languages) laments. Pawel who moved to Melbourne and married a quiet woman from Korea who lived next door. Meanwhile, you and I slowly climb the Tower of Babel without a map.

# Family Reunion in the Old Country

Zosia left the foothills of the Tatra mountains and never came back, but her granddaughter did for the big family reunion. It started with a Mass in a consecrated grotto and ended at four in the morning with a drunken bash complete with a raging bonfire and big bottles of beer. The family priests weren't around for this part. And this is how her people must have celebrated before the coming and going of any priest: drunk with beer and each other. Starting orgies in the fields to make sure there was a harvest, enough to eat, enough healthy mouths to continue the family line. Listening to the moon for any last-minute instructions.

# Man Praying in a Field

He could be dead, this man praying in the field between Warsaw and Poznań. He doesn't merely kneel, but places his whole body against the body of the earth; listening for some small breath to match his own. People must have prayed this way before the idea of God forced them into small country churches and ornate urban cathedrals. Before pulpit and incense and the creation of man on a ceiling in Rome. Here is only hard earth and a man lying down to pray. He wears a dark suit, black shoes, his hands open in supplication. The coarse wild grass he worships hides his face. Soon, dusk will approach and call his name. Only then, will he rise from his prayer as if startled from sleep. Barely remembering who he is, he will walk away— each foot lightly blessing the ground.

## Meeting the Famous Poet in Kraków

Just simple, keep it simple, my friend advises me. No elegant summer dress with fashionable strappy black shoes. No chiffon scarf caressing bare shoulders. He wouldn't notice anyway since he lives and breathes words. Not the thing, but the idea of the thing. So a denim skirt, heavy sweater, and a golden amber pendant to ward off the deep gray Kraków sky will suffice. And don't go to lengths explaining why you are here; he wouldn't believe it. Just stick to the facts. A mother, a father, and you. He might claim your mother is a perpetual orphan. He might accuse your father of being a fraud. But he cannot say anything against you, since you give him no cause for alarm. Only a book of poems you wrote on the other side of the world. Small words that clothe the soul, not the body. They will speak to the silent white rooms of his apartment as soon as you are gone.

# Hel as a Destination

Not the fire and brimstone located in some frenzied minister's Sunday sermon, but here: on this skinny sliver of a peninsula northwest of Gdańsk. It juts out into the Baltic Sea as if it was sleepwalking one night and forgot what it was. Land or an afterthought of ocean. Here is where the first shots of WWII were fired: the small garrison of Polish troops held off the German Nazi invaders until they didn't. The rest really is history. In the new century, war is finally over—for the time being—and Hel settles into its second life as a tourist hot spot. Hiking trails, restaurants, numerous jewelers selling amber. At the water's edge, you can see a fake pirate ship, The Baltic Roger, owned by an entrepreneur from Stockholm. His employee, a man on the dock dressed as a pirate, urges the tourists to sign up for a dinner cruise complete with seven courses, champagne, wenches to serve the meal, and a talking parrot. True history buffs would be scandalized until they looked closely at the pirate. His scars are real, his missing right arm in the empty sleeve pinned over his heart is not computer generated. Try to imagine the color of his eyes: blue of sky, green of sea, brown of earth? Or all of the above?

# Malbork

In the main chapel of the Malbork Castle, the one built by Teutonic Knights, straight through a chancelet window—miraculously through the thin glass—a branch of ivy tentatively reaches in from the outer walls. A living testament of how life, however unlikely, can survive death and destruction. This castle has seen so many assaults through so many centuries: if not by the Swedes, then by the Lithuanians and Poles; if not by the Pope, then by time and neglect; if not by the Nazis and Soviet army, then by Communism and unbelief. Four months before the end of World War II, the red bricks of Malbork Castle stood until Hitler and Stalin decided to play feudal war lords from January to March in 1945. Within two months, they destroyed almost the entire castle complex. Today, even the Grand Master of the Teutonic Knights could not envision the brilliant green ivy growing into the chapel wall—oblivious to the odds against it.

# Dark Green, Forest Green

The young performance artist carefully opens the envelope from Hong Kong with her green—dark green, forest green—fingernails. Perfect color, perfect application. Her thin wrist is tattooed with a band that looks like a beaded bracelet my daughter would carelessly wear and lose. The artist moves her hands as if they were leaves on branches. The green so vibrant a small sparrow would be forgiven to mistake her for a tree. Meanwhile, the letter in the envelope waits: its words mixed with the scent of dusk and birdsong.

# The Daughter Draws the Pines of Rome

The daughter who rarely talks to her mother sits in the Colosseum, surrounded by the silence of the past. She likes the indifference of history, the cool reticence of the ancient marble that has witnessed so much pageantry and spectacle, so much pain and blood, but still maintains its distance. A distance she doesn't have to bridge. From her vantage point, she can see a grove of Roman pines across from the amphitheater. The archway perfectly frames one particular tree. As if the monument's anonymous architect placed his building at this intersection of stone and air just to capture the tree for this woman in the distant 21st century. In turn, she tries to capture it on the empty page of her notebook. The pale white comes alive with her pen and ink sketch: the thin trunk, the symmetrical umbrella of dense branches. She draws the tree as an answer to the question she knows her mother will ask back home.

# The Crazy Girl in Łódź Who Thinks She's the Slavic Reincarnation of the First Mrs. Rochester from *Jane Eyre*

Even though she lives in Łódź, the Hollywood of Poland, she's never seen any movie of Bronte's novel. And she's never been married either, but that doesn't stop her from going crazy and sequestering herself in her mother's attic. Or, the "third floor garret" as she calls it. She, in this case, being the mother since the daughter is as mute as a wall. "Where did I go wrong?" the mother laments while the father stares at his hands. While the silent daughter points to every crack in the ceiling on the hour—as predictable as clockwork—in her room just under the roof. She likes the view of the street: there, so close to the sky she could lick it if she wanted. But she doesn't want much. No friends, no lovers. Only the steady drip of water: from a faucet or a cloud, it makes no difference. She still listens to the drops. At night, when everyone's asleep, she leaves the attic and walks through the house. She knows every nuance of chair, table, cold tile floor with her eyes closed. In the basement, she sleeps with her head against the white-washed foundation. When she dreams, it's always the same dream with her voice doing the narration...

*I forgot to turn off the stove. I'm sorry. And now the kitchen is gone. I'm sorry, I'm sorry. Fire. Fire, everywhere. Even when it's not burning, I still smell it. Glorious sulphur—the yellow mixed with orange and blue. I see a match and it makes me cry. On TV, I saw a pop singer with sparks sizzling from her breasts, her crotch, and it made me cry. I will donate my eggs to any woman who has no ovaries. I will listen to every root growing in my mother's garden. I will promise to never wake up.*

## Sabbatical

He imagines winter as a harsh wind off the Baltic coast. Or the gray sky tattered as if it was ready to split open with stark branches of oak and willow, the silence of absent gulls and breathing. At the very edge of his field of vision, stands a woman with flaming red hair almost covering her entire face. Her chin is resolute like a border crossing, but her mouth is cursed with deep lines, no smile, no frown. Her lips want to escape the anonymity of her face and go somewhere else: a café, a street corner, a train, a dirt road in the countryside. Anywhere but this empty coast and its silent waves that never reach the shore.

Crazy spring. Crazy for coming to this small village where all the smoke from the houses collect into one cloud. One cloud that barely covers a green sky and the multi-colored wings of an angel announcing nothing. The artist imagines this scenario as if he were Fra Angelico the Surrealist. No Byzantine halo for the angel but wings of amber and scarlet, turquoise and amethyst, garnet and citron. A faint smile. Somewhere, rumors of a resurrection, of a fresh start, a breath of new life. But here, he sinks into the gossip of the imagined angel that parts the low hills with its wingspan. This crazy place where his wife—she of the smoldering cigarette—was born.

In summer, clouds live in the lake. The water so calm it can be as cliché as a mirror. But he doesn't want cliché as he struggles to make the shock of white terrorize the concept of blue. But what do all these colors mean: the colors in multiple tubes living an easy life in his cramped studio? What happens when he confronts the clouds, the lake, the mirror? He doesn't even know and he's supposed to be the Full Tenured Professor, the Man in Charge. All he wants is the canvas to be complete: the scene to appear miraculously in front of his startled eyes. A perfect landscape of muted tones that knows him better than he knows himself.

## Postscript: Autumn

In autumn, he doesn't paint what surrounds him: the landscape stained with dying colors that fade from gold to shadow, from crimson to hint of movement. He paints what has eluded him—the anonymous figure, a woman seated in her nudity. The body so unblemished it breathes in the empty canvas and exhales parted legs, shaved pubis, a blank face, an open gash where the head would dream. His dream has nothing to do with what he sees, only what he desires: the distant future where an art collector in a foreign country discovers this painting in a damp basement and catches her breath. Weeps.

# Adrift

The collector's house is cluttered with art. Picasso reproductions. Chagall in a strange frame of raw cedar. Rare poster art from Poland before the Nazi occupation when children went to the circus. Abstract landscapes of bare trees. The house is as cluttered as the bus that delivers the tourists from America. They arrive jet-lagged and adrift.

The collector makes sure her guests are well fed. She presents three tables filled with the work of her own hands: the cucumber salad with sour cream and dill, the spice bread laced with slivered chestnuts and apples; the slender wraps of chicken and ham. The pressed red wine: floating rubies touching their lips.

The noted art historian is late for his presentation. The tourists mull around the buffet and try to ignore the clock. Their collective circadian rhythms collide with its chimes as they mimic the church bells of Westminster. Or are they St. Michaels? Or Whittington? Or some foreign place where their American voices are silent?

Finally, the end of their long day. The art historian arrives, the food is consumed, the ruby wine glows in their throats. The collector shows them her prized piece: a seated nude, a woman devoid of all possessions except what the viewer imagines (the historian explains). "Really?" asks the widow from Nebraska.

# The Sacred and the Profane in Toledo and Seville

When she saw El Greco's masterpiece, *The Burial of Count Orgaz*, in the chapel of Santo Tome in Toledo—the painting consuming one entire wall—she did not notice the Virgin's brilliant red and blue robes, only the evocative hands and black cloaks of the noblemen that reminded her of the dark gypsy dancing the flamenco in Seville: his hands like two birds—starlings at dusk—floating above her body.

## Arriving at the Train Station, the Last Place I Saw Lara Alive

It looks the same, but it doesn't. Death clouds the eyes—not with tears—but with the fog that comes with loss. You can see the train platform still there in the center of Vienna, in the center of Europe. But the faces are different: hers, gone. Look...she was young, younger than me in her yellow linen dress, the color of a muted Viennese sun, and her fashionable white hat. Her husband, the distracted older man, was standing with her on the platform waving goodbye. That was then. Years ago, when she could still lift her arm in welcome or farewell. Now, no trace of our embrace at the station. The sleeveless summer dress, the pale arms. The spacious apartment she slept in, on the street where a deaf Beethoven composed his last symphony. Now, it's vacant and empty. All part of memory's passing blur. The train arrives, the train departs. The city remains. Only the faces have changed. Her husband has moved on to another station. And I (the friend left behind)—I, too, have moved on: the passenger lost in fog.

# Scattering the Ashes on Lake Geneva

He plans the memorial exactly one year after she died. The quiet death in Brussels that left him alone. She died while he slept, while the whole city slept: a single tear in the corner of her eye. He tried to collect it in a linen handkerchief before it could evaporate, but what good would that do? She was already part of the air. Better to think ahead, cremate the body, and plan for the memorial service far away. She wanted a lake and a lake she will get: the cold and pristine waters from the Alps in Lake Geneva. Geneva of the expensive lipstick. Geneva of the UN diplomats with security badges and pressed suits. Geneva of the hushed rain where he first met her, that woman who is now being scattered on the lake's calm surface. For a long time, she does not sink. Her ashes cling to the surface, asking one more question of the current under him.

## The Cloud Sleeps on the Mountain

Just outside Segovia, its heart embraced by the Rio Eresma and the Rio Clamores. Just outside the city, its cavernous cathedral of gilded chapels and vaulted ceilings filled with immense air and light. Just outside its expansive Alcazar, the castle growing from barren granite as if sheer rock dreamed itself a new persona cloaked in the fairy tale of a trapped princess. Do you see it? The mountain beyond the valley, as transported from another dream. The heavy mist covering its silent gray head, as if a cloud just escaped the mouth of God to find peace, to fall asleep, to escape that roiling imagination.

# Foreign Subplots

*House of Strong Light—El Escorial*
Philip II builds a monastery near Madrid with over 2000 windows. It's designed like an upside down grille because the place is dedicated to St. Lawrence who (legend has it) was burned to death on a gridiron. His famous last words: "Turn me over, I'm done on this side." When the sun sets on a clear day, the monastery's windows fill with fire.

*A Herd of Butterflies Near a Manor House—Scunthorpe, UK*
As if their delicate bronze and black wings could even faintly resemble the appendages of cows or bison or goats or sheep or anything else that moves in herds. But the travel-weary tourist from upstate NY just blurts out the first thing that comes to his mind. The fluttering gemstones covering six forsythia bushes don't care.

*Primitive Art Above the Main Altar in a Museum that Used to be a Church—Holland*
The city is forgotten, just like this church where only art lives now (not God) and primitive art at that. Mary riding a blue unicorn, Jesus flying a kite, Joseph striking a pose with his hammer and nails. Let's not even imagine what the angels are doing.

*Oak Tree Growing Out of a Skylight—Near Minsk*
"Just a sapling breaking loose from its acorn prison," says the village philosopher who sells goat cheese on the side. She wraps each wedge in green cloth that imprints its weave on the hardened skin: tiny leaves embracing each bite.

*Young Man Whose Face is Covered with a Birthmark in the Shape of a Cloud*
He sits with his parents and a beautiful woman—girlfriend, fiancée, lover, wife?—in a posh restaurant in an exquisite city in the middle of Europe. Let's say, east of Paris; let's say, west of Kyiv. Let's say he's bored as he peruses the menu filled with minute descriptions of dead plants and animals. Nothing surprises him anymore. Not even his reflection floating like a nimbus in the mirror across the room.

# Pablo Picasso in Lucerne

The rich society dame that dreamt-up this museum must have had one helluva crush on the bald Spaniard. Everywhere you turn, there's nothing but his huge ego in gallery after gallery. Every now and then, a contemporary of The Great One shows up unexpectedly: a lost Miro wandering through the blue period or a Calder mobile hanging by a thread among the body parts of mismatched women. And, speaking of bodies, where is the dull husband of our rich patroness? Perhaps he's trying to resemble a series of cubes floating down the stairs. Or an angry bull reduced to a bicycle seat. At any rate, he's desperate for attention. He's certain his wife is having an affair with Picasso's ghost. Her moaning in her sleep is a dead giveaway. In the morning, she looks right through him to gaze at the white wall staring back at her. The perfect canvas for his attempts at reproduction.

# Love and War in the Park, Lucerne

The middle-aged couple sitting passively on the stone bench have no use for this flagrant display of fluid desire that engulfs the park. Two other couples—one quite younger, one quite older—"go at it" like they're competing in *Double Jeopardy*. Any minute the convivial host will appear with the final answer. Meanwhile, the Japanese tourists take countless pictures of the Lion chiseled on the side of a huge stone outcropping. The symbol of Switzerland's defiance against the dreaded French in some long-forgotten siege, the Lion is skewered with so many arrows even Cupid would be amazed. It's war, not love. But try telling that to the strident exhibitionists with their French kisses and dry humps. Not one of them is interested in a truce. The embarrassed couple on the bench must decide the winner: neutrality is not an option. They only want to disappear into the sculpted facade. To become the Lion's closed eyes, his barely beating heart.

## The Judge from Central Poland

Another day. In the morning, eight civil weddings to sanction for the state. One couple stands out: an army sergeant with gray eyes whose uniform is weighted down with medals; his bride in a mint green dress, curling-ironed bangs, a red poppy corsage below her left shoulder. They both look nervous, don't even smile when the brief ceremony is over, and a friend snaps the mandatory photo. In the afternoon, an easy case. A small-time punk (in 1950 he'd be called a capitalist hoodlum) roughed up and robbed a frozen food delivery man in an alley behind a restaurant in Warsaw. Open and shut, guilty as charged, five years in the provincial prison. The judge's fate is not much better. A long commute to the outskirts of the city. A cold dinner of blood sausage, cabbage, and parsley potatoes with a distracted wife. Her face reflected like cut crystal in his glass of chilled vodka.

# The Eve of St. John the Baptist's Feast Day, Warsaw

Tonight, no unmarried girls in this city desire husbands. "Get a husband and you get trouble," a mother warns her daughter. Tonight, I came to the edge of the Vistula River expecting to see its waters ablaze in light: light from hundreds of flower wreaths set on fire by anxious young girls hoping to get married. All day long, they wear the wreaths of wildflowers on their heads as if their hair grew naturally entwined with lupine and chicory, Queen Anne's lace and daisies. At dusk they remove their wilted crowns, light them with matches, and set them adrift in the water— praying that the small burning circle will float (and foretell marriage) and not sink (and foretell spinsterhood). But tonight, in this new millennium—no girls with innocent wishes, no fires in the river. Only a loud and raucous music festival complete with beer, cigarettes, and a rented band from Britain playing American country and western. At the edge of the crowd, a man in the shadows caresses his lover and, with his tongue, licks her perfectly arched white neck.

## On the Side of the Road

No, not in Gdańsk plying their trade on a busy street. But in the forests of rural Poland, flaunting their tiny black bras for the truckers and tourists on the lonely two-lane highway from Warsaw to Łódź. Forgotten and bruised women with bleached hair, short skirts, high heels that never leave their feet as they raise their legs to fuck the businessman from Berlin. Later that night, he will watch the hardcore porn channel from his silent hotel room. Pretending he's still screwing that whore in the woods, he'll imagine that's him in the orgy scene. He won't notice the male actor's ugly face, the oiled tits of the horizontal blonde. How her body accepts anything—cock, tongue, dildo—without complaint. The next day he will get lost in Poznań's old market square. Miss the day's big event: the medieval clock with its two mechanical goats butting their heads at noon.

# Still There

Twenty years later, there's only one prostitute, one *dziki kobieta* (wild woman, as my grandmother would describe her) waiting for a car to stop and make her job less predictable. She embodies the colors of the almost-perfect virgin: tiny white dress, tiny white chair, tiny white cell phone. The dark woods of oak and willow behind her listen in on the conversation.

# At the Zeitgeist Hotel, Vienna

The tram's brakes outside your window screeching like battle cries of Teutonic Knights.

The toilet flushing sounds like a 747 landing at a small airport where the runway is too short, where the terminal is cloaked in fog.

The large pink and white peonies, their fragrance, the scent of your grandmother returning to her country of origin, the hapless Hapsburg Empire.

Dreaming of your dead mother and her large dresses printed with unknown blossoms, unknown colors that haven't been invented yet.

The waiter as a teapot, as your dead father, short and stout. One hand on his hip, one hand cupped to his ear, waiting to hear you decide on the fate of your lunch: clear broth with spaetzle or the mysterious daily special—the red-eyed fish from an unknown sea.

Eating your dinner: the heart and lungs of a wild boar in the hotel's restaurant, *Kulture*.

The chartreuse parasite, leafy and full, growing on the trees outside the door. Doesn't matter what trees—each of them covered in the same color.

Bleached moose antlers above the doorway of a modern building down the street. They radiate a whiteness so pure, the sun is intimidated.

Honor system wine bar on the corner near the squatters' park. Never a broken bottle. Every empty carafe of Riesling, Rosé, Malbec recycled for the next journey.

Sexworld in a tiny museum on the other side of the train station: a permanent collection of anatomically correct dildos from all over the world. The exhibit from ancient China's Tang dynasty leaves patrons speechless.

Eternity in the small effigy of a dead child housed on a page of a medieval art brochure. Full color, no caption, the grieving parents don't inhabit the space.

The stern mountain folk and their narrow God encased in a rural shrine. On either side, red and yellow wildflowers imagining the palette of the first day.

The nearby cathedral with its wooden Christ that pilgrims lick. Not even the tears and hair of the New Testament's reformed prostitute cleaned his feet so well. They glisten in the approaching dusk.

The silent statue of the Blessed Virgin Mary, alone in the choir loft of a gray stone church, somewhere east of the city. Heat from the votive candles in the forgotten side chapel. Prayers for the living and dead: you among them.

## Painted Toenails in Ukraine

The young girl who gives the American woman a pedicure in the town's most elite spa, doesn't know the difference between a foot or a knee. The woman doesn't want to embarrass the girl and her lack of English vocabulary, so she never corrects her. "Other knee, other knee, other knee," is the mantra the woman sporadically hears as the right foot and then the left is covered with green kelp from the Black Sea and massaged into her skin's oblivion. Other than the incorrect word, the girl is silent. A thin gold Orthodox cross dangles from her neck as she daydreams about her lover's thigh. She paints the woman's toenails in such a hard, brilliant red that, weeks later, no nail polish solvent can remove it. The woman will have to wait a year—after the nails have totally grown out—before every trace of the color is gone. The girl and her halting mantra, a silent echo.

# Lipstick in Geneva

She's been in this situation before: the dilemma of buying lipstick in a foreign country. Then, it was Warsaw—now, it's Geneva. Back then, everything was cheap in Poland before the EU and foreign investments. Now, everything is priced sky-high in Geneva to keep up with the secret bank accounts and mansions, the Mercedes and Jaguars with black-tinted windows. A hamburger is $35. A simple salad is $50. And that ultimate tube of vanity—lipstick—is $75 a tube. Yes. $75. And not in some pricey boutique but in a corner drugstore. $75 for Christian Dior's *Diorific Lip Colour*: Mystic Mauve and Cancan Orange are the same steep price. No color better than another. So what's the foreign wife to do? Pucker up and pay or risk having her lips disappear amidst Geneva's well-heeled, well-dressed women? As she contemplates her face in the mirror, the sunset glows coral and crimson just behind her.

## The Maid from the Hotel in Białystok

It takes her all day to make a bed. First, she strips it down to the mattress pad and lets it air out. The bed needs to breathe—she says—breathe so that it can forget all the dreams left behind from the night before. The professor from Lublin with his visions of stone bridges; the banker from Warsaw with his pounding heart; the widow from the mountains who takes the spring's snowfall wherever she goes. How can the empty bed forget—their hair, their skin, the imprint of their bodies? The maid knows only time holds the answer. Several hours after stripping the bed, she puts down the fitted bottom sheet. Several hours later, she smooths down the top flat sheet. Another several hours pass before she covers the bed with a large comforter smelling like the green of her backyard after the rain. And, finally, she places the square pillow with careful precision at the head of the bed, exactly in the middle. Only then is the bed ready for the next dream: the dark rooms of an abandoned house that haunt the quiet bureaucrat from Moscow whose wife is as constant as a blank page.

# Café de Paris, Switzerland

The restaurant serves one entree with two side orders—steak, salad, and french fries—that's it. No need for menus, no need to read French or Italian or German, no need to stutter with an American accent. The widower from Brussels at the next table had a wife who was a vegetarian. She wouldn't be caught dead in a place like this. The smell of the meat would be enough to put her over the edge. She's dead, so it's a moot point. But her husband still dreams her alive. He remembers (like it was just last week) how she berated him for eating a greasy hamburger. Not because it was greasy, but because it came from a cow. Just like the quiet cows that dot the Swiss countryside outside Geneva. Just like the cow he's eating now: medium rare, slightly bloody. His wife hated meat but approved of the ancient world's ritual of gazing at slaughtered animals' entrails to predict the future. He envisions her frown appearing in the reflection of the red juices pooling on the plate. Her mouth opens in disbelief: *What do you think you're doing, eating in a place like this that doesn't even know what tofu is? Think of your heart. Your congested, breaking heart.*

## Visiting the Valley of the Fallen, Spain

At the grave of Generalissimo Franco, we argue whether or not there was a Mrs. Franco. Or did he merely have a mistress like Hitler and Mussolini. Or was he sexually dysfunctional: akin to having Hitler's one testicle (the other one a shrunken marble that never fully descended). Or a dysfunction that reflected another weird Hitler anomaly. My father's theory ("hey, I read it in *The New Yorker*") that Hitler, as an adolescent—and on a dare—put his penis in a goat's mouth to urinate. When the unfortunate goat bit his penis, causing a rather primitive circumcision, Hitler started hating Jews and then started to formulate his Final Solution. I swear. That's what my father believes. And we stand before Franco's tomb and laugh about history and its crazy back stories, the hidden alleys we crave to walk down.

## Pornography at the Charles de Gaulle Airport, Paris

In the airport store the wife sees—right next to the tour books on Algeria and Cyprus—the pornographic DVDs. A big-breasted brunette with an open blouse and a policeman's hat glares suggestively at her husband, the former priest. He's oblivious to her breasts. Just as he's oblivious to the wide-angle naked butt of the woman sharing the shelf with the busty policewoman. "The Bare Secrets of Tatiana" looks tame enough: a shaved pubis with black garters coupled with a vacant stare straight out of the Urals. What to do with a man who is too busy looking for aspirin and cough drops to notice "Lola and Her Big, Thick Throb." His wife remembers seeing a naked woman on a beach in Tahiti. A real naked woman, not some dirty postcard. She was standing just yards away, hosing herself down at a public shower. Her husband was taking a picture of a fishing boat and missed the naked Tahitian completely. By the time he turned around, she was already wrapped in a towel.

# His Wife Gets Profiled at the Zurich Airport,

along with the teenager from Albany, the retired schoolteacher from Dayton, the lawyer from Phoenix, the grandmother from Omaha, and the pregnant woman from Seattle. No rhyme, no reason, no sustained and rational narrative. Just a "get out of line and surrender your passport." In a makeshift screening room—a heavy black drape suspended like a shower curtain in one corner of the gate area—they are paraded one by one and asked to describe the Hudson River, Wright Brothers, Colorado River irrigation policies, insurance claims, and Starbucks. His wife gets a multiple-choice drill. Their eventual status has nothing to do with watch lists, terrorism, or bombings and everything to do with geography, history, politics, economics, and the proper amount of foam on a decaf latte. Our heroine's husband is frantic. He refuses to board the plane until his wife emerges victorious from behind the black curtain. What happens next is anyone's guess.

## The Diplomat on the Flight from New York to Amsterdam

He's the only passenger to order wine on the 9:30 AM flight and he keeps spilling his Cabernet Sauvignon on his blue nylon jacket. Good thing the jacket is a dark color to sabotage any stain. Good thing the jacket repels any absorption of permanent damage. But he keeps wiping the spilled wine with his tiny Delta Airlines napkin. Is he pre-occupied by the thought of blood diamonds in the Congo, ivory poachers in Kenya, his father's lungs collapsing in a Johannesburg hospital? Or maybe he's thinking of his wife in Mombasa: a strict Muslim who might suspect what he was doing 35,000 feet above the Atlantic. His left hand holds the plastic cup as the gold ring makes a slight imprint on his perfectly manicured finger.

# The Dead American Poet in Rome

The dead American poet in my dream still smells of life with his white suit, fashionable cane, and steaming espresso. He sits at an outdoor café on the Via Veneto as if he's waiting to be discovered by Fellini for an engaging Italian sex farce set in the late '60s. Book awards and Guggenheim Fellowships were never enough, so this dream is his best shot at stardom: thousands of women screaming his name. Once, I wanted to be one of those women—infatuated and hoarse. But that was in the boring realm of reality, not the here and now of the ephemeral dream. Here, he merely amuses me. Now, I walk to his table and show him the latest edition of *Il Tempo*. At the bottom of the front page, a small blue car balances a large white sign on its roof. It looks like an ad for a pizzeria, but it's actually an obit. The black letters float in the warm Italian air. The poet's eyes try to focus on the name. "Guess who?" I ask him in the muted voice of the dream.

# Arch Made of Codfish: Hammerfest, Norway

A guy lives in a small dot on the map. To ease the boredom, he likes to make ridiculous claims about love: how it's responsible for global warming and the subsequent demise of the polar bear. To stay consistent to his train of thought, he compares the affection he has for his wife to loving a carp, a codfish, or a clam. The metaphor is filled with bottom feeders: from the green-brown carp with its fleshy whiskers; to the dull red cod and its FDA-approved liver oil; to the burrowing gray foot of the two-faced clam. Is that any way to love a wife? To keep bragging about the never-ending seafood buffet? Imagine him in cumbersome waders, trying to reel in enough fish to construct an arch, a bridge, a convenience store, a town. "Look, look," he says to the wife in equal tones of excitement and disbelief. "All this silver losing itself in the dry sun. Just for you."

## The Tourists Get Their Rental Car Stuck in Cannero

Such an embarrassment in northern Italy: the Lake District filled with large tourists in tiny cars. Or in this case, small tourists in a big car. No matter the details, they can't find their hotel—a small boutique number on the shores of Lake Maggiore. Not as crowded as Como, but they still drive past the front door and the bewildered locals who can't imagine *where* they could be going with that car. Creeping down the pedestrian lane, ignoring the universal road signs (an outline of a car with a stark red line slashed across it), they take a left turn onto an even smaller road. Narrower than an alley, a footpath, a bicycle lane. The car gets stuck between a bar and a pizzeria. They can't move an inch until a kind waitress rushes out, gently frees the side mirrors, and directs them to drive in reverse down the steep path they just came from. They disappear with their car, the buildings streaked with black, black scars.

# Postcards

The Russian waiter in Ryazan with his dyed shirt looks like a blue-patterned teacup—chipped and worn—with his hand on his hip, waiting to take my order, as if I were Pavlov's salivating dog.

The Sistine Chapel is a study in facelifts: all the centuries-old dirt and soot cleaned away from the skin of Adam, the cellulite of the Delphic Sibyl, Zechariah's sagging neck, the furrowed brow of God.

The soft wind in the field near Zagreb as a ballroom dancer covered with purple lupine, yellow goldenrod, and the small white boneset that can never remember its name. Hush: the wind is singing—a quiet waltz, the movement of stems and light.

The toilet flushing in Prague sounds like a jet ready to take off from LaGuardia—overpriced, overrated drone: too many tourists from China pushing the handle, rushing from the stall, washing their hands with foaming soap that doesn't rinse fast enough.

The church in Breda as museum, as gallery, as an atheist's dream—all oil on canvas, gilded frames, abstract sculptures that twist the air into marble hair—no room for water, wine, Madonna, child, the idea of God hovering like a red light above the empty altar.

The cypress trees in this Italian landscape feel like the green of my childhood, the line of green separating our tiny suburban yard from the world; as if the trees were sentinels guarding a cemetery that hadn't been invented yet, the living still living.

The dream of my husband in Vienna as a prologue to a movie, *The Third Man* in three acts—his dead mother the main character (not Orson Welles) in a flowing blue caftan as diaphanous as the sky, ready to ride a Ferris wheel at dusk.

The large peonies bursting with fists of pink and red taste like pure heaven to the ants who ravish the blossoms in my grandmother's garden: in the foothills of the Tatra Mountains, their scent is as strong as memory, her empty arms, a closed door.

## The Gift

On the other side of the world, she buys him a tie the color of burnt sienna; the color of the soil that surrounds La Mancha. Not the color of impossible dreams and windmills, but of soft clay she can mold with her hands. Oh, how she misses his mouth: kisses of the night wind that touch her skin. She will startle his with muted shades of earth that will embrace his neck when she returns.

# Doppelgängers

For as long as it takes the woman in Kyoto to write a prayer, a litany of words, a laundry list of desires, you will have finished your cigarette in the bar in Vienna that sells Australian beer. For as long as it takes the man in Ishikawa to eat his sushi off a naked woman lying on the buffet table of a fashionable restaurant, your wife will have finished ironing the spotless white shirt she bought on sale at a Sears in Des Moines.

# Stadtpark, Graz

Early March and the hyacinths are already in bloom. Vibrant yellow and muted lavender surround the overbearing fountain—a gift from Vienna in 1873. Loud derelicts—drunk on cheap beer and themselves—chase stray dogs and each other. A Buddhist monk discreetly appears from nowhere and takes a sequence of photos with his iPhone: a bare cypress, red graffiti on a cement wall, two Pomeranians digging in the dirt. He is wrapped in an orange robe with gold trim. For him, there is nowhere but here. This windy day in southern Austria where the drunken man with purple hair sings a dirge filled with love. Or lost love. Or almost love. Or never love. Like this neverland nestled in a map near the Slovene border. Maybe the monk asks the quiet sycamore, "Where am I going?" Its branches filled with no clouds and a pale blue. He spends an hour waiting for an answer. Anybody's guess, he guesses. And the answer would be totally right and totally wrong, depending on where you are at any given moment. Meanwhile, the shadows of the dogs and the drunks collide.

## On Leaving Seville

The immense green plain blossoms into one solitary tree; its top branches filled with stork nests, as if it possesses flat hands that open effortlessly like wings to hold the long-necked birds feeding their young so casually, it makes the sky weep.

# On the Other Side of the World

*After the Funeral in Seville*
Two sisters go to a flamenco bar after they bury their father. They sit silently with their cool Agua de Valencia and watch each dancer as if they've forgotten sorrow and all its mismatched relatives: grief, mourning, the black scarf with white pearls. They're only aware of the dancers' feet pounding the floor, the insistent guitar, the bare arms twisting like branches of a willow tree. Each branch ends in a flurry of leaves. Each leaf cradles the twin shells of castanets. Their dark, ebony faces.

*Statue of a Woman with Broken Serpents Embracing Her*
She's totally forgotten in this Kraków park with its endless parade of harried students clutching cell phones and stoic grandmothers carrying plastic bags filled with potatoes, fresh dill, and coarse salt. Nothing harried, nothing stoic about her: the Anonymous Woman cloaked in the blue patina of broken serpents. They cover her breasts and pubis, thighs and feet. The Madonna of the Underworld? The Anti-Virgin of What is Holy? Even the sculptor refused to name her. Keeps her eyes open, her mouth closed.

*The Train Station, Vienna*
The old woman wears a fashionable purple beret and collects free newspapers from three different kiosks in Vienna's main train station. She would be a bag lady in the States, but her scarf is too perfect. Its universe is serenaded by flocks of black starlings perched on bright yellow trees. What more can be said about the landscape she wears around her neck? Or the man on the train passing into the night who sees it?

*The Horseradish Dish*
Somewhere in Bucharest or Budapest (a place Americans can't find on a map) she finds the one restaurant that serves fresh grated white horseradish. When the waiter brings the spice to her table, she's startled to find its pungent fragrance trapped in a little coffin of pure glass. "Be careful," the waiter whispers, "what you wish for."

# The Priest's Garage

He doesn't own a car. Next to the small church, attached to the large spartan rectory, across the road from a statue of a little-known saint from Bohemia—the garage sits empty. John Nepomucene, the patron saint of the confessional, chose to be drowned in a river rather than reveal to a jealous king his innocent wife's confession. John N. whose silent tongue was miraculously preserved several centuries after his death. Our rural priest is no saint, but he's married to a vow of poverty: why have a car to distract him? As illogical as television or a camera phone. So he walks, takes the train, rides his bicycle. "The old black crow on two wheels," the village boys laugh behind his back. When the rich relative from America comes to visit, the priest offers him a quiet room with a view of the overgrown orchard. And the empty garage for his rented Peugeot. The garage smells of rain, old paint, turpentine: smells that remind the American of his grandfather's garage in Chicago. The immigrant that never learned how to drive.

# The UFO in Katowice, Poland

Yes, it's landed near the center of the city: a Soviet-era saucer that Stalin built on a tilt to house sporting events and rock concerts. Years later, the Vatican will compose top secret documents to explain the existence of aliens if they land in St. Peter's Square. The Catholic Church wants to cover all its bases with *some* protocol in place, just in case. My friend, the atheist, thinks it's all a joke: the Vatican, the aliens, the ugly UFO arena. *Who can make sense of anything except the rational non-believers? Soon, mathematical formulas will prove everything—even the nonexistence of the soul. And the ultimate myth of free will. And why children die and wonderful things happen to rotten people. You can't explain any of this with God.* So says the atheist from Katowice as she dismisses the UFO in the middle of the city and sleeps with her dead mother's crucifix hanging from the bedroom wall.

## The Infant of Prague in Prague

In this unexpected place—where 85% of the locals profess no faith in anything (no god, no goddess, no multi-armed Shiva offering comfort)—it's almost a shock to see The Infant in his royal regalia. Turquoise velvet cloak, aquamarine satin dress. In a side altar enthroned in a church in Prague, The Infant holds reign in this city where most people claim he doesn't exist or ignore him. His mother isn't fazed one bit. She casually stands in a corner to his right—her outstretched marble hand presents him to the world, as if saying: "Here he is! Here's my boy!" like any proud Jewish mother. My mother had a thing for this particular incarnation of this incarnate God-Son. She volunteered to host another elaborate statue of The Infant of Prague from the local church in Cleveland when the pastor announced a special month of devotion. Families signed up to keep the statue for a week and my mother was one of the first. She placed Mary's boy in the center of the mantelpiece in the living room. Every day she washed, dried, and ironed his clothes. Honorable work, she thought, for any mother.

## Seeing My Daughter's Face on a Wall Covered with Saints in the Priest's Rectory, Kraków

Holy cards and family pictures. The sublime and the mundane. The stigmata of Padre Pio and the unsmiling Saint Faustina. Blessed Klinga and Pope John Paul II. Saint Peter in chains and Saint Paul with a sword. The blessed Virgin with her yards of blue drapery and Saint Mary Magdalene, former prostitute, naked except for her floor-length hair. Saint Lawrence on his grill and Saint Sebastian pierced with arrows. Saint Agatha and her bleeding breasts and Saint Maria Goretti with her halo. Dozens of nativity scenes and Christmas cards from around the world: Australia, New Guinea, Guam, Ghana, the Virgin Islands, Chicago, Mexico City, my mother's suburban house near Cleveland. The newborn Christ, the shepherd Christ, the tortured and dead Christ, the Christ resurrected, the Christ ascended and transfigured. And there, almost unrecognizable, tucked between an angel with huge wings and an unknown saint holding an open book and a flaming heart—my daughter, the agnostic, smiling.

# The Skinny Tour Guide from Spain

He's been a tour guide for the UN headquarters in Geneva for five years and it shows in his ever-shrinking waistline that can barely make decent conversation with a belt. It's on the very last notch, and it's still too loose. He complains to the tourists about the cost of food in Geneva: a small meal of soup, salad, and tea—95 Swiss francs. No wonder he's so skinny; he can't afford to eat. His mother in Salamanca worries that he's anorexic. Whenever she visits from the plains of central Spain and sees his body sinking deeper and deeper into his shadow, she weeps. She weeps and brings food: paella, tapas with beef, pork, and saffron rice, flan. Nothing piques his appetite. After years of "starving to survive" (his euphemistic turn of phrase), he's forgotten how to eat. And when he remembers, his body forgets and just throws it back up. His mother's love staining the white walls of his small bathroom.

# Fake Tex-Mex

The long drive from the mountains of Jelenia Góra to the green valley around Bielsko-Biała and nothing to show for it but a fake Tex-Mex restaurant called "Indiana." The place looks like a huge wine cellar that just happens to serve burritos that could double as jumbo gołąbki and enchiladas verdes that are more red than green. But isn't any Mexican restaurant outside the borders of Mexico fake? Some more than others. Like the one on the outskirts of Ishpeming in upper Michigan. No Mexican in sight— only Swedes and Finns—but that doesn't stop the blond owner from opening a taco bar. He pipes Ricky Martin in the restrooms and can't tell the difference between Acapulco and Guadalajara. All this means nothing to the southern Poland border town surrounded by hills and fog. A buck is a buck. A peso is a peso. A złoty is a złoty. Only the name changes.

# The Street Cleaners of Kraków

They are performance artists who can't find "real jobs," as one of their mothers emphatically states, stirring her tea as sugar the color of new snow melts in the cup. But her son feels no regrets as he reinvents himself every night on a small stage in a dark bar

*It's just an awful cellar filled with cigarette smoke and bad girls who should be home with their parents, the mother interrupts*

near Sławkowska Street. He lives for these smoke-filled nights: the unrehearsed performances with his comrades-in-arts (not "arms") where he can become anything. A tiny snowflake caught in the hair of a woman from Wrocław. A wedge of goat cheese from the market in Nowy Targ. A Chicago pizza with a fetish for mushrooms. Even the tips are decent—enough for a shot of Żubrówka, his favorite vodka, complete with a thin blade of bison grass sleeping in the bottom of the bottle. (One night, he even got to perform as the bison). A great night is when the artists—all three of them—have enough tips to buy the whole bottle. Then another performance begins. After the bar closes and the night still owns the early morning hours—the three men don't sleep. They become their alter egos, the street cleaners of Kraków, complete with costumes (white jumpsuits) and props (long handled brooms). This transformation is just another part of their ever-expanding repertoire. Not as pitch-perfect a performance as morphing into the choir of blue jays arguing on the banks of the Vistula. But close.

## Where Do Famous Dead Writers Go?

Here's a joke—the day before Easter, he dies. He, the famous writer who once called me a "poetess" to my face. (He emphasized the "tess" as in *Tess of the d'Urbervilles*, a novel he probably regretted he didn't write). My husband said he meant it as a compliment, but I doubt it. I saw him again years later in a swanky restaurant in London—disheveled and drunk, wearing a brown leather vest that smelled of old Chardonnay, menthol cigarettes, and cheap perfume. He didn't recognize the poetess, but he did recognize my cleavage: the breasts in middle age still symmetrical, still perfectly divided into northern and southern hemispheres, the trajectory of his tongue. He wanted that tongue to leave the language of the earth, howl like the yellow wolf of heaven, and disappear into lightning.

# Dijon Mustard in a Toothpaste Tube

No joke about it. In Geneva—where the international movers and shakers spend their days in countless meetings and their nights in countless cocktail lounges talking about the meetings—simple gestures are disguised. The handshake masquerades as a worn stone. A glance becomes an x-ray. A silent wave of the hand is ephemeral as a cloud reflected off the lake. So it should be no surprise that dijon mustard (not the plain yellow stuff on any ballpark hot dog but the Grey Poupon found in only the finest limousines) comes in tiny toothpaste tubes in this city where the League of Nations crashed and burned. The perfect camouflage—just like everything else. Six degrees of separation in Geneva: League of Nations; United Nations; One Nation Under God; God Bless America; American as Baseball, Apple Pie, and Hot Dogs. *Do you want mustard on that dog?*

## The Rude Russian Women in Lucerne

Everybody hates them. Even those neutral, laid-back Swiss who never take sides against anybody. But these two women are different. Loud. Obnoxious. Constantly smoking. Insulting the waitress in the Rathaus Café who is stuck serving them endless glasses of iced vodka. They make faces behind her back, curse the food in low, guttural Slavic grunts—but eat every crumb. They could be distant cousins or close friends or mere acquaintances. Hard to tell, since they basically ignore each other except when joining forces to complain about everything: the too-pure Swiss air; the too-pristine mountains; the too-perfect lifestyle of this landlocked country that has rarely seen war, has never truly suffered. But neither have they—the young, faux rich of the New Russia. The Siege of Leningrad is nothing more than a forgotten chapter in an unopened history book. Why waste their holiday visiting the war monuments in Moscow or the tired family dacha in the Urals? They're entitled to the whole world and anything in it. Even this peaceful "piece of shit country in the middle of nowhere."

# The Hunchback on Isola Madre, Italy

His back is bent and stuffed into a thin blue jacket with a broken zipper. He doesn't say a word but has a chronic cough. The younger man in the orange shirt that accompanies him is curt and gruff. Yells at him to "andiamo" and, otherwise, ignores him. When the hunchback reaches the stunning botanical gardens surrounding the Villa de Borromeo, he sits on a bench and smokes. Doesn't pay attention to the red azaleas, the rhododendrons, the wall of camellias and its cascade of pale faces. Not even the huge Kashmir Cypress, the largest in Europe, gets a glance. Halfway through his cigarette, a white peacock approaches him, and with a shrill cry, spreads its glorious plumage. He's tempted to blow gray smoke into that cloud of feathers and see how the peacock reacts. With surprise, with anger? Would the cloud disappear into the early evening sky? Before he can find out, his young companion starts to complain about catching the last ferry back to Stressa, the smoldering cigarette, the hunchback's annoying habit. The roots of the giant cypress hear the coughing as the tree's Oriental needles fall like rain in the gravel courtyard.

# Trapped

The drunken woman from Brighton navigates the stairs and accosts the American student on the landing. She is in Italy for the first time (the American, that is) and has no time or patience for the tipsy Brit who's too old, too drunk, and too obnoxious. *Pain-in-the-ass-waste-of-space*, the college kid mutters as the woman tries to grab her arm to steady herself. *Dearie, sweetie, luv.* Those affectionate nicknames don't work on Ms. Coed. Mrs. Brighton might as well be a brick wall or a disingenuous piece of art at The Royal Pavilion—that kitschy, tourist trap in her home town. Would the American ever come and visit? *Hell no*, the student thinks and keeps on climbing the stairs to the third floor and her small room overlooking Perugia's Umbrian hills. But the next afternoon, when the American gets stuck in a public water closet in the 93-year-old hotel and cries out for help from

*anybody, anybody at all, please get me out*

it's the Brit from Brighton—still old, still drunk, still roaming the halls—who somehow springs the door open. A fluke? A coincidence? *Oh luv, just consider me your guardian angel*, she gushes to the embarrassed American who is quietly elated and only wants to kneel in thanksgiving and embrace her feet.

# Homesickness at Krynica

She must be American—with her spotless hiking boots and bright fuchsia lips—but what is she doing here in Krynica, the biggest spa town in Poland? Most tourists don't know about the pristine mountains, manicured trails, and special mineral water that tastes like pearls. "If pearls had a flavor," she writes on a postcard to the sister back home. She's not interested in hearing about the six varieties of water and what they supposedly cure: anemia to sour stomach, dull complexion to colitis, sinus congestion to ear wax. The woman only wants to hear a familiar American accent. When a man from Chicago stumbles over Polish diphthongs, she almost cries at the mispronunciation of *dz, cz, sz, rz*. A blessed blur of sounds leaves his lips and travels to her yearning inner ear. "Your health," she raises a glass of Słotwinka in his direction and hopes he notices.

# Amber Museum, Gdańsk

She had no idea that an amber stone could be as big as a boulder. Or it could reflect hundreds of different shades of white, green, yellow, cognac, red. Had no idea early Christians believed these colors were a direct result of The Great Flood. The tears of dying children: pure white or perfectly clear amber to wear as ornaments. The tears of repentant sinners: cloudy and marked with dark veins that could be burned as incense. The tears of the guilty—the greedy and arrogant, the merciless and unjust—all their tears became black amber that had to be destroyed: useless and cursed. Pagans also imagined creation myths for amber: ant feces, elephant semen, the swollen genitals of ancient giants. All the myths—holy and mundane—exhibited in a museum. Dangling from her ears, enclosing her wrists, encircling her neck. Her life, surrounded by myth.

# The Irish Guest at the Wedding in Kraków

She is loud, loves to drink and smoke, and she's living in sin with a man from Gdańsk. A man who should know better, according to his mother, the quiet woman with swollen legs. But what can she do? She's no match for the Irish mouth who speaks broken Polish—perfectly. This mouth confronts me about my life and realizes I have a husband...who's a doctor. "Well, aren't you the lucky one?" and "Does he give free medical advice...for this?" At that exact moment, when the band just finished playing an oberek, the Irish guest lifts up her dress to expose a long scar from her last C-section. "See this?" She shows my husband, shocked into silence. "What can you do about this?" She whispers as she fingers the deep white line—a roadmap from Galway to Kraków—and describes every step. From yellow gorse to Mazovian willows; green cliffs to Baltic shore. From her dead mother to her dead son.

## On the Train to Breda

The little yappy dog on the stylish woman's lap has no passport or national allegiance; he barks at local citizens and foreigners alike. The old man with the round, horn-rimmed glasses looks like George Burns or my Polish grandfather. He's upset about the price of tickets and tries to engage the female conductor and another passenger in his debate. But he's old and they don't want to get involved. He finally shuts up, dons a straw hat with an orange band, and gets off at Rotterdam. The young Dutch student notices us and moves to sit across the aisle. Fluent in English, he teaches us about the geography and history of his country as the flat landscape blurs past. We're barely paying attention ("look at the groves of poplar trees") until he talks about the rise of fascism in certain countries and I describe the small but vibrant Jewish community in Kraków. They refuse to leave, to emigrate to Israel or America; they refuse because they are home. Their children take klezmer lessons and perform in the Tempel Synagogue with a heartbreaking wail of clarinets that silences the student.

# The Passenger Next to Me on the Flight from Kraków to Chicago Who Looks Like My Mother

Same bulky frame, same arthritic knees, same thin hair dyed honey blonde and teased into tight curls. The exact same coiffure my mother demanded every Saturday from her favorite stylist at Marcelletti's Beauty Salon in Maple Heights, Ohio—the boring working-class Cleveland suburb. The exact same stylist who burned my scalp when she cascaded my hair into French curls with a too-hot curling iron. Such torment I endured for a Senior Prom with a boy whose name I can't even remember. All I can remember is my throbbing scalp and the emerald-green ribbon that the stylist wove into the French curls to distract me from the red blotches. Emerald green to match my prom dress, to match my birthstone. The same green that this stranger is wearing: deep green that reflects the fields of Poland, that reflects my absent mother's eyes. She sits stoically, eating pretzel sticks and nodding a smile to me every now and then. Oh, Mother, you were never close to me—whether sitting on a plane or in a silent, suburban living room—as you closed the door between us. You're buried far below the clouds outside the plane's window. Window that's open only to the sky.

## Her Daughter in Love in Paris

It's Marie Antoinette. No, another woman with big hair. No, an erratic butterfly of bright orange and deep black with the silhouette of a woman's face emblazoned on its back. Is this what love has done to her daughter? Made her retreat into a cocoon until she emerged like Venus on her scalloped shell? Complete with sea spray, tangled hair, fragile wings she doesn't realize she has.

## The Girl Among the Hydrangeas

Not even two, she barely speaks the language—any language—as she's dwarfed by white hydrangeas. Her face surrounded by large spheres of blossoms that rival any cosmic starburst. But she's indifferent to the laws of astrophysics or botany: indifferent as the flowers are to her presence, her touch. Her father takes a video. Not the daguerreotype of old Paris—muted, strained, the young girls starched into their sedate lives near the Tuileries Garden. But the flash of the digital world. The new millennium girl adrift in the color and sound of bending the long green stems, rubbing her cheek against the white gift they offer. The father intent on capturing her before she's gone.

# Memory as Red Hibiscus in Santorini

The surprise of it. The shock of red hibiscus that the Greek tour guide picked and gave to me in Santorini. Santorini: my daughter's favorite island also reflects the name of my favorite aunt. Santo Irini, Saint Irene, Aunt Irene— my mother's youngest sister and the best. But here is this brilliant red handed to me by Eleni, the tour guide whose name embraces my mother and my daughter. Eleni, Helen, Ellen. A name that derives from the Greek word for light. I knew this when I named my daughter in the middle of a Perseid meteor shower on the eve of the Assumption of the Virgin Mary: one of the most important holy days in Greece, rivaling Easter and Christmas. The day when (as the believers believe) Mary was assumed into heaven without having to go through the trouble of dying or burial or decay. This woman from Nazareth who retired to Ephesus, revered by the Greeks as their favorite saint. Mary, Irene, Helen, Ellen. All the women in my life claim this island's light, the deep blue of its sky, the deep red of this hibiscus.

# Bone Country

The next night, I dreamt I was in a huge forest and the branches of the trees were like broken arms, the sunlight throwing their shadows on the forest floor. I saw nothing but the green air of the trees. I heard nothing but the low moan of the wind. Finally, from the edge of the woods, came a soft sound: the voice of my grandmother—my mother's mother, the one who died before I was born. She was singing in a language that even the trees could understand. She was singing and calling my name. Telling me that I was in my bone country: where my mother and father could not follow, where only my heart would know the map.

# Everything in Poland is Two Hours Away

Kraków to Nowy Sącz, Rzeszów to Katowice, Malbork to Gdańsk, Sopot to the Hel Peninsula, Tarnów to the Ukrainian border, Hitler to Stalin, the Polish Corridor to the Vistula River, Pomerania to Białystok, Warsaw to the edge of the primeval forest, the border with Germany to the border with Belarus, here to there, past to present to future, my life to my death.

# The Cemeteries Near the Ukrainian Border

The dead are orthodox. They want cut flowers arranged in perfect bouquets above their hearts and freshly starched bows of white linen attached to their gravestones. Even the mourners have to pay attention to protocol. Heads must be covered, hands folded in prayer, no distracted gazes to the right or the left. The dead are always in your face, up close and personal. "Don't you dare forget us," they demand. And the old women near the Ukrainian border never do. On market day they buy extra bread then cross the San River to the cemeteries. They cover their gray hair, anticipate rain. Toss small crumbs filled with rye and poppy seed amidst the crowded crosses, the rusting crucifixes nailed to trees. They watch the blackbirds take the bread to heaven and pray that the dead will eat and be satisfied.

## After the Thunderstorm

—*for Zbigniew Herbert*

After the thunderstorm, a glaring sun and devastating blue sky fill your city. After the thunderstorm, only old men with talking parrots entertaining the tourists. After the thunderstorm, percussion groups from Warsaw perform *West Side Story* on vibes, drums, and xylophones. After the thunderstorm, buildings are rebuilt according to the original medieval plan and people return to inhabit them again—to live, breathe, love, hate, die. After the thunderstorm, we eat special noodles cooked with chipped beef and buttered mushrooms. We drink iced water and strong beer. We're given an exorbitant tab for the meal, but pay without complaint. After the thunderstorm, we don't mind. After the thunderstorm, we don't care about history or consequence. Only about love: who has it and who doesn't. After the thunderstorm, we marvel every day at the rising of the sun, the clarity of the moon, the distant brilliance of the stars. After the thunderstorm, we keep looking at our hands to see if we're still alive. And, yes, by the smallest of miracles, we are. We are.

# The Night's Blue Bowl

My first night home, I dreamt of you and your daughter. Happy and reconciled after so many years of forced silence. Unlike the waking world where a whole ocean separates you: mother on an island surrounded by aquamarine; daughter far away on a thin peninsula of intangible green. The muted gray of air, your only common denominator. But, in the dream's world, the landscape's edges fall away, leaving nothing but dusk. Bird song. Thin burst of sunset. Deep cobalt of the night's blue bowl. Laughter. A young girl quietly holding your hand. A single line of pure horizon connecting everything.

# Acknowledgments

I would like to thank all my mentors and friends who have supported my work throughout my career: Lisel Mueller, Ellen Bryant Voigt, Stephen Dobyns, Faye Kicknosway, Colette Inez, Maria Mazziotti Gillan, Therese Becker, Miriam Pederson, Jack Ridl, Rodney Torreson, Diane DeCillis, Pam Luebke, Anne-Marie Oomen, M.L. Liebler, Leonard Kniffel, Richard Jansma, David Cope, John Guzlowski, and Ewa Parma.

Deep gratitude to the amazing staff at Cornerstone Press: first and foremost, Director and Publisher Dr. Ross Tangedal who accepted *Bone Country* for publication; editors Brett Hill, Grace Dahl, and Maria Scherer, who were so professional and meticulous with their close reading of the manuscript; and Julia Kaufman and the press production team for designing such a beautiful cover to put the finishing touches on this book that has been so close to my heart from its first inspiration to its last page.

I am especially grateful to Kathleen McGookey, for her generous comments as she was the first to see *Bone Country* in its early drafts; to Stuart Dybek, Matthew Gavin Frank, Clare MacQueen, and Leslie Pietrzyk for their wonderful endorsements. All five of you have been members of my literary dream team for years. I'm honored.

Special thanks to my family: Brian, Stephanie, and Lyla Foster; Ellen Foster; Deborah Nemec and Joe Cirincione; and the late (and great) Pete Foster.

And, my deepest thanks to my husband Tony: dearest confidante, friend, lover, and traveling companion extraordinaire. My journey would not have begun without you.

Gratefully acknowledged are the editors of these magazines and journals in which the following pieces first appeared or are forthcoming, some in slightly altered versions.

"Postscript: Autumn" in *I-70 Review*

"Arch Made of Codfish: Hammerfest, Norway" in *CHEAP POP* (online)

"Bone Country" in *DMQ Review*

"The Cemeteries Near the Ukrainian Border" in *Dunes Review*

"Café de Paris, Switzerland" in *Earth's Daughters*

"The Maid from the Hotel in Białystok" in *Inch*

"Portrait of the Dead" in *Kritya* (online)

"Dark Green, Forest Green", "Love and War in the Park, Lucerne", "His Wife Gets Profiled at the Zurich Airport," "Tea in Istanbul", "Conjuring Her Face", "Gemini Marks the First and Second Hour", "Flight to Warsaw", "Scattering the Ashes on Lake Geneva", "The Eve of St. John the Baptist's Feast Day, Warsaw", "Amber Museum, Gdańsk", "Doppelgängers", and "The Girl Among the Hydrangeas" in *KYSO Flash* (online)

"The Street Cleaners of Kraków" and "The Judge from Central Poland" in *The MacGuffin*

"Planting Geraniums on Geranium Street", "On St. James' Feast Day, the Shells of Abakanowicz", "Indigo Sky Above Spain", "Tower of Babel", "Pablo Picasso in Lucerne", "Dijon Mustard in a Toothpaste Tube", "Lipstick in Geneva", "Memory as Red Hibiscus in Santorini", "The Infant of Prague in Prague", "The Priest's Garage", "The Irish Guest at the Wedding in Kraków", "The Night's Blue Bowl", "Adrift", "The Muslim Wife at the Best Western, Zurich","My Husband Disguised as a Stranger in a Kraków Bar", "Hel as a Destination", "The Cloud Sleeps on the Mountain", and "Foreign Subplots" in *MacQueen's Quinterly* (online)

"Abandoned House in the Tatra Mountains", "House of Strong Light—El Escorial" (from "Foreign Subplots"), and "The Tourists Get Their Rental Car Stuck in Cannero" in *Michigan State University Libraries Short Edition*

"Somewhere in Europe, Surrounded by Villagers, a Bride Leaves Her Home", "Arriving at the Train Station, the Last Place I Saw Lara Alive", and "The Passenger Next to Me on the Flight from Kraków to Chicago Who Looks Like My Mother" in *Paterson Literary Review*

"In the Perfume Store, Kraków" in *Peninsula Poets*

"On Leaving Seville" in *Reformed Journal*

"The Daughter Draws the Pines of Rome", "Painted Toenails in Ukraine", and "The Dead American Poet in Rome" in *South Florida Poetry Journal* (online)

"Man Praying in a Field", "The Waterfall in the Mountains", "In the Old Town, Warsaw" in *Witness*.

---

"Café de Paris, Switzerland" (titled as "Café de Paris: Geneva, Switzerland") was published in *The Blue Divide* (New Issues Press, 2021).

"The Irish Guest at the Wedding in Kraków" was selected for inclusion in the *2022 Best Small Fictions Anthology* (Sonder Press, 2022).

"On the Other Side of the World" won second prize in the Flash Fiction Contest sponsored by Fish Publishing in Ireland. The piece was published in the *Fish Anthology 2022*.

"The Hunchback on Isola Madre, Italy" and "Stadtpark, Graz" were published in *Contemporary Surrealist and Magical Realist Poetry: An International Anthology*. Jonas Zdanys, editor. (Lamar University Literary Press, 2022).

"Gallery of the Street" was a finalist in the *River Styx* Microfiction Contest (2020).

"Tower of Babel" was an honorable mention in *New Millennium Writings'* Flash Fiction Contest (2019).

"Scattering the Ashes on Lake Geneva" was nominated for the *Best Microfiction Anthology* by the editors of *KYSO Flash* (2019).

"Conjuring Her Face" was nominated for the *Best Microfiction Anthology* by the editors of *KYSO Flash* (2018).

"Arch Made of Codfish: Hammerfest, Norway" won third prize in *CHEAP POP*'s Microfiction Contest (2015).

"The Cloud Sleeps on the Mountain" was nominated for *Best Spiritual Literature* by the editors of *MacQueen's Quinterly* (2022).

"Abandoned House in the Tatra Mountains" was adapted into a short film. This film was selected to be featured at Filmetry, an international festival sponsored by Michigan State University (2022).

*Bone Country* was a finalist for the 2021 Off the Grid Poetry Prize and a selection of the manuscript was a semi-finalist for the 2022 Tomaz Salamun Prize.

---

Wisława Szymborska's quote preceding "Tower of Babel" originally appeared in the *New York Times Magazine* article "A Poetry That Matters" (Edward Hirsch, 1996).

Linda Nemec Foster has published twelve collections of poetry, including *The Blue Divide*, *Amber Necklace from Gdańsk*, *Talking Diamonds*, and *The Lake Michigan Mermaid* (2019 Michigan Notable Book), which was created with co-author Anne-Marie Oomen and artist Meridith Ridl. Her work appears in magazines and journals such as *The Georgia Review*, *Nimrod*, *New American Writing*, *North American Review*, *Witness*, *Verse Daily*, and the *Best Small Fictions Anthology 2022*. She has received nominations for the Pushcart Prize and awards from the Arts Foundation of Michigan, National Writer's Voice, Dyer-Ives Foundation, The Poetry Center (NJ), *Fish Anthology* (Ireland), and the Academy of American Poets. The first Poet Laureate of Grand Rapids, Michigan (2003–2005), Foster is the founder of the Contemporary Writers Series at Aquinas College.